*The Little Guide to Social Avoidance*

**Irene Graham**

s u m m e r s d a l e

Summersdale Publishers Ltd
46 West Street
Chichester
West Sussex
PO19 1RP
UK

www.summersdale.com

Printed and bound in the EU.

ISBN 184024 276 0

To be a successful social avoider you need to be plotting, scheming and a good liar. You need to remember your excuses and not get mixed up with things that you said you were doing to get out of doing something with somebody else. Phew, it's a tough call.

If you ever get the opportunity, request to come back as a cherished domestic cat (cat-flap non-negotiable). Your social avoidance will be admired as an endearing haughtiness. You can dip in and out of people's lives knowing that you will never be rebuked for enjoying your own company so much.

Text messaging may seem like a good communicative medium for the social avoider but don't be deceived: its see no one, hear no one, speak to no one philosophy may seem heaven-sent but text messaging quickly escalates to meetings in person. Text messagers are desperate for social participation – avoid them at all costs.

Cars are a total giveaway that you are at home (based on the correct assumption that you don't walk anywhere). So if you have a garage always keep your car in it therefore suggesting that you are out if anyone calls. If you have a garage but no car, hide the entire family in it until your house-callers have gone. If you have a car but no garage, park it out of view of the house or in the nearest supermarket car park. Alternatively, replace your car every week.

No matter how environmentally friendly you are, refrain from using public transport. The inevitable close physical contact gives some people the go ahead to enter into trivial chatter normally restricted to couples who have been together for too long.

Only go out when it is raining. The legitimate use of a hood or an umbrella is the perfect way to avoid the pistols-at-dawn routine of oncoming pedestrians.

**Don't send birthday or Christmas cards. This is a quick and efficient way of removing extraneous people from your life – especially overly sensitive ones.**

When you do engage in conversation with someone, avoid any eye contact. Instead, frown at a distant place just above the left shoulder of your companion. This really pisses people off. They won't come back.

If you wish to study for a degree then choose a long-distance learning course so you never need enter the social pressure cooker of a university.

Have you ever felt jealous when someone has had to leave a party early to get back home to their dog? Using a pet as a reason to depart is more acceptable to people than announcing that you have reached your social saturation point.

Try not to work in a place that has allotted times for communal morning/lunch/afternoon breaks. If you are unfortunate enough to have to work in a place like this then spend your entire break behind a broadsheet newspaper (see if you can get them in large print and the paper might come in marquee size). This is not a great tactic if your social phobia causes any trembling in the limbs as a quivering paper is bound to attract more attention (stick it in the freezer an hour before if possible).

If you have to attend a social function such as a wedding, christening or funeral and it would be inappropriate to use all the usual avoidance excuses, then, if female or a social phobic cross-dresser splash out on a hat with the largest diameter brim that you can find. Don't worry if the chapeau does not flatter your face – as long as it casts a shadow over your knees then it will be a supreme tool in social avoidance.

Invent yourself a very demanding dog who cannot be left for too long as he pines and chews all your furniture - then you get to leave the party before you chew off all the skin on each of your fingers.

**Choose to see a film at the cinema on one of its last days of screening: with any luck there will only be you and the bloke on his own with the family-sized popcorn.**

# When going to the theatre, book tickets for four people and then go on your own.

Don't wash for long enough and you will have a visible personal space that no one will want to enter.

# Don't engage in small talk – it is a social hobby with folk.

Take to riding a motorbike and then you can wear your helmet to avoid possible verbal skirmishes. I know that you probably think the motorcycle courier looks like a complete ★★★★★ when he walks into a building clad in leathers and a helmet but do you ever see him passing the time of day with anyone? No, so keep your helmet on and your visor down (even if you don't have a motorbike).

Talk about yourself
all the time … on second
thoughts, maybe not as this
is considered normal
conversational etiquette by
the majority of the
population.

# Only have one topic of conversation: your bowel movements and how to promote them.

Become a lighthouse
keeper in the world's
tallest lighthouse.

Invent an illness that can be used as an excuse for all those do's you would rather not be doing. Be careful in your choice of complaint, as you will invariably come across an empathic sufferer who wants to discuss with you in detail their symptoms, contra indications and treatments. Before you know it you will have signed yourself up for 10 sessions of acupuncture for your pseudo complaint.

Having children can thrust you into the glare of many unwanted social situations. These include: eye contact through rear mirror of car with other waiting parents at school pick up; birthday parties; 10 friends round for a sleepover (they are not the problem – it is the parents who come to pick them up); the fear that your child may grow up to become a social attractant and ruin your hermetic existence. Unless you can invest in a nanny to carry out all the less desirable functions of child-rearing then seriously reconsider this lifestyle choice.

People tend to gravitate towards their own parameters of what they perceive to be 'normal' so try and look so outlandish that you will be beyond anyone's boundary of acceptance (as long as it doesn't cause you too much distress when you look in the mirror).

# Your choice of transport should be a lorry with a 'carrying nuclear wastes' sign.

Have tinted, triple-glazed windows throughout your home (of course this includes the garden shed where some folk may sometimes find their only retreat).

Try and choose a partner who is an only child. This will reduce the possibility of family get-togethers and all those social obligations that you didn't consider when you eyed your partner over a crowded dance floor. Or hook up with someone who has no family living within a 50,000-mile radius. Also, move 50,000 miles away from your own family.

At work, strategically place a plant with a large leaf surface area on your desk so as to obscure your view of colleagues. With the clever use of office paraphernalia such as your monitor, printer and lever arch files you will be able to construct a verbal shield around you (with the added bonus of them not knowing when you are getting no work done).

When going into hospital the social avoider does not dread the operation but the enforced communal living. Fellow patients like to swap alarming stories concerning their medical condition but you should frequently use phrases such as 'I've never felt better' and 'Pain is all in the mind' to guarantee solitude.

Carry a bleeper round with you as part of your job (poetic licence may be required if you are a window cleaner) and get it to go off at timely moments when you have reached your social brimful.

Move to the place in the world where there are the fewest hours of sunlight as sunshine can have a devastating socialising effect on people. But bring along a light box, as you don't want light deprivation to spoil your isolated bliss.

Team sports, the gym, aerobics and suchlike are no-go areas for the social avoider. So if you feel like you are not getting enough exercise install a large trampoline in your back garden and bounce away. This could backfire if your neighbour finds the intermittent appearance of your head over his fence entertaining and calls everyone over for a laugh.

When searching for holiday destinations ignore holiday guides and the recommendations of friends. Instead, visit places that no one has ever heard of – it will be worth the six flight changes.

Don't recharge your
electric toothbrush.

Spend your life
underneath a 15 tog
(duvet cover optional).

Join a religious cult that promotes vows of silence and solitary confinement. Suicide pacts are optional if you want to take social avoidance to the extreme.

# Don't ever enter the *Big Brother* house.

Beware of mobile phone spotters – they are curiously bold if they hear a phone melody they like or you have a phone with a feature that theirs lacks. You can be certain that they wouldn't come over and help you if you fell over in the street but will gaze lovingly at your phone like they have been friends for years.

If you must submerge yourself in water, dunk in a flotation tank rather than go through the ordeal of alligator watchfulness in a swimming pool.

Work from home -
even if you are a door-
to-door salesperson.

**As well as a 'No Canvassers/Salesman' sticker on your front door you should extend this list to include unwanted family and friends.**

Smokers have some unfair advantages: they get the best seats in restaurants (at the back of room quiet and secluded); they have regular breaks at work to escape from unbearable office banter; they are boycotted from some people's houses or made to smoke in back gardens away from the rest of the group. If you don't smoke, take it up – even if it means using a substitute such as a roll up filled with organic multi-purpose compost.

Live in another country and don't bother to learn their language (even if it is your own mother tongue).

For privacy in the garden use fast growing conifers and settle the neighbourhood disputes when at least you can't see them.

# Use a pogo stick for everyday use – ideal for avoiding eye contact.

When you go out with friends get drunk, argumentative and on the way home throw up in their car.

Refuse to laugh at people's jokes – even if you find them funny. This may require the use of facial muscles that have previously lain inactive.

If aged over 30 say that you still live with your parents (even if you are married with 4 kids) – people's judgmental sensors are curiously heightened by this choice of lifestyle so you can guarantee to be dismissed as being 'a bit strange' and your quest for social isolation moves up another notch.

If you are short-sighted don't have corrective eye laser surgery. It is appropriate for the social avoider to view the world as a foggy mass and be oblivious to all the eyeballers. If your 20/20 vision doesn't allow you this comfortable option then wear corrective glasses and this will give you the same blurry effect.

Play video games 24/7. This is a sure way for people to start not wanting to be around you – the amount of aggravation this will have on people is directly proportionate to your age. Make sure you just have one controller to prevent other video gamers joining you. The social avoider is not a competitive person.

(For younger people this activity has the potential to be a social attractant so ignore this advice if you are under 30).

Before a football match, covertly attach a piece of Velcro to the football and your football boot. Throughout the game you will have permanent contact with the ball but be unable to score a single goal or pass the ball. You will need to be convincing in giving the impression that great skill is required on your behalf to maintain such intimacy with the ball. You will not be invited into the communal bath after the game.

**Never wear your underwear on your head in public places (although this is a desirable activity just think of all that attention).**

Hope that the burkha
makes it onto the catwalk
this year.

When socialising, only go to fancy dress parties ... as the invisible man.

Order everything from catalogues.
Granted, you will spend the majority
of your life returning unsuitable goods
but at least you won't have to wade
through the human traffic full of
people who are actually shopping for
pleasure and not because they
desperately need to renew the black
pair of trousers that they have been
faithful to for the last 5 years.

Use your answering machine wisely. It is not to be used to retrieve messages when you return home but to filter messages whilst you are at home. When you don't feel like talking to anybody display your feelings on your pre-recorded message. A suggestion: 'Hello, I am here but I don't want to speak to anyone right now but leave a message and I will get back to you when I am feeling a bit more sociable.' If you have reached your people saturation point for the year and it is only January then be more direct: 'Piss off. I know who you are and I don't ever want to talk to you again.'

**When going to the beach, always bring a windbreaker with you even if the air movement has gone on strike. Extend the use of this social decoy for other situations such as queuing for the January sales.**

Sunglasses are very useful to hide behind but you need to be careful as they can promote other people's scrutiny: you may look so beguiling in them that you are irresistible to watch. Beware of people who wear sunglasses because they think it makes them look more attractive as they will try and catch their reflection in your sunglasses, which can be a bit disconcerting for a social avoider.

Become a temporary worker and never stay in the same job for more than a couple of months. This timespan allows you to be detached from the rest of the workforce as your imminent departure curtails their efforts of friendliness. Just think, you need never go to another work Christmas party ever again.

Whenever someone tries to discuss anything serious or personal with you, start making animal noises and this will prevent anyone getting emotionally dependant on you. The choice of animal is completely up to your embarrassment threshold and vocal range.

Whenever you enter a new building immediately familiarise yourself with all the emergency fire exits and then use them as your normal entry/exit routes. But don't get yourself stuck in any lift shafts in pursuit of a people free passage out of the building.

Work nights in a lunchtime-opening
sandwich bar.

# Sod Off!

Christmas is certainly an ordeal for the social avoider. A few festival shirking hints:

- Tell everyone you are doing voluntary work in a soup kitchen and book yourself into an atheist hotel for the week. The fib is necessary as people think it is abnormal to want to be by yourself on Christmas Day and they will force you into accepting an invitation using torture methods.

- Completely succumb to family pressure and enthusiastically accept every Christmas dinner invitation from different family splinter groups so avoiding the autumnal wrangling about where you are going. Then ring everyone with a feigned illness just about the time the turkey is being basted.

- Tell everyone that you will surprise the younger generations by coming as Father Christmas then pay someone to go in your place. Beneath all the ho-ho-ho-ing, the padding and the silvery facial hair no one will notice that it isn't you. Just make your decision of stand-in carefully - not someone who will flirt with your mother.

If attending a work
presentation ensure
all your escape routes,
which you will need to use
once you have been in
there for 5 minutes, have
been sussed out . Make
sure you are not sat next to
another social avoider as it
could end up in an
attention-rabbing scuffle
out of the door.

Don't feel that you are not living up to your social avoidee credentials if there are certain people that you actually enjoy being with for extended periods. But do get concerned if these moments last for more than a couple of hours. If you must support a football team make sure you support a local team from the bottom regions of the league. Watch them play mid-week away matches at the other end of the country which will ensure a low turnout. You won't get many football highs but at least your lows will be in exile.

Before you enter somebody's house, ensure that the soles of your shoes are generously covered in canine excreta.

# Get married by video conference link so you don't need to be in the same room/country as your guests (and possibly your future spouse).

Pretend that you have lost your long-term memory after a severe bump to the head. This will give you permission to ask the question that you have wanted to ask certain people for years: 'I'm sorry, do I know you?'

If travelling by air, get yourself
padded out in XXXL clothes.
You won't fit into the standard
seat and there is a good chance
you will be accommodated in the
quieter surroundings of business class.
But be prepared for possible humiliation
when you collapse under the strain and
rouse to see disapproving eyes above
you watching the bubble wrap
unwinding from your shirt.

Move house every six months.

GOD
OFF!

**Speak in a stream of senseless gobbledegook in an earnest and sincere way.**

Don't put yourself on public display by pavement jogging. Use a treadmill indoors with some four-star in the oil burner and traffic sounds on the hi-fi to recreate the ambience.

**Warn every visitor that your house has been condemned by the council for asbestos.**

Drive to the nearest busy road and explain on your mobile that you were on your way to the party but your car has just broken down and you will try your best to come but it depends on whether it is fixable (no chance). You won't get away with using this excuse if it is your neighbour's party.

If you are sat adjacent to a keen converser on a train and they have interrupted your book reading and gate crashed your personal stereo listening then resort to pretending to be asleep. Dribble to make it look more realistic. Just make sure you don't miss your stop.

Grow a long fringe (tickling your upper lip sort of long) and use it as a facial curtain to protect your privacy as you would with any other curtain. So draw it fully if you want to blank everyone out (a good idea on the Tube). Slightly open your curtain if you want to have a look around just to make sure you're not sat next to the man/woman of your dreams. If you feel like you want to go to the next stage and fully draw open the curtain then get your fringe cut.

If you have always had a desire to perform on the stage but your social phobia has prevented this then consider dramatising as the back/front end of the pantomime quadruped.

Have a walk-in freezer built into your home so you need only go out once a year. Be prepared for opposition if you share your home with other people as they will certainly see better uses for such a project such as a conservatory, en suite, decked barbecue area etc.

No matter how talented you are as a singer, actress, dancer, musician, laboratory technician etc you must repress your expertise as fame and social avoidance are incompatible states.

If you are one of a pair of identical twins then let your more confident, extrovert, attention-seeking twin stand in for you for all those social situations that will be dreaded for weeks by you but looked forward to by your sib. With any luck they may like your life so much they want to stand in for you permanently.

Live on the 100th floor of a tower block and take up a new hobby – lift sabotage.

**Have a camcorder on hand and simulate filming - this will part the waves of Saturday morning shoppers a treat.**

Adapt the idea of the annoying car alarm that talks to you to protect your own personal body space. 'Back off from me! You are coming too close! Keep away from the face!'

Have so many botox injections that you end up with no facial expression. A numb stare is a wonderful social decoy.

Confuse a garlic
clove for a garlic bulb.

# Discover the secret of eternal youth ... and then keep it to yourself.

Forward yourself as a volunteer for the Moon Colony Development Programme.

**Try and use camouflage techniques for merging into the background. (Wallpaper suits don't need dry cleaning either.)**

Live on a canal boat – as long as you have a higher tolerance level towards ducks than you do towards people.

# Wear a T-shirt saying 'Cannibals have rights too!'

If people ask you to guess their age it means they think they don't look it – add a decade onto your estimate. They won't get too friendly with you.

Win a million quid and then give every penny to a hedgehogs in distress sanctuary. A long-standing friend who is about to get his house repossessed will be so pleased for the prickly beneficiaries.

Put in a personal injury claim against someone who psychologically disturbed you by maintaining an uncomfortable amount of eye contact with you on the train.

If you are really bad at doing something you should do it alone so as to avoid attracting any attention. For example, if you need more than two manoeuvres to park your car in the supermarket car park then park in a nearby quiet street. Rather than negotiating the kerbs with your trolley get a taxi back to your car.

**Adopt an involuntary bodily movement and you will find that people will give you more than your usual amount of personal body space.**

In the office keep your telephone head set on and just pretend that you are talking to someone to give you a break from both customers and colleagues. But remember not to continue doing this once you have removed the head set.

Go to your careers adviser
and ask for information on
becoming a shepherd.

**Train as a magician and make people disappear or yourself disappear, whichever is most preferable.**

Some people have corrective surgery to remove excess skin from their eyes. You should ask for a pair of horse blinkers to be put on.

Society in general finds it hard to accept that some people are not naturally social and prefer their own company. People take it as a personal insult if you choose not to be with them. Sociability is valued whereas the freedom to choose to be alone is seen as being eccentric or dull. It should be stated in every employer's equal opportunities policy that: 'We will not discriminate against people who choose to spend their lunch break on their own and choose not to socialise with the rest of the staff in their own time after work.'

Reveal a friend's most intimate secrets when in a group. This will ensure that you won't have to listen to his or her outpourings again.

**Money can't buy you happiness but it can buy you social avoidance – so keep gambling on the games of your choice.**

Train in army commando tactics as there are so many that are useful in social avoidance. The commando-style belly walk is brilliant for escaping from any number of social events.

# Be a subject bore. Choose a subject that the least number of people will be interested in and talk at length. But don't underestimate people's desire to join a group otherwise you may find yourself president of your local 'different ways to water your garden' society.

Come clean! Out yourself
as a social avoider so you
won't need to use this book
for excuses!

Forget the portrait-sized photo – have a life-size blow-up doll who is a rubbery version of yourself and take it everywhere with you and talk to it constantly.

**Become a missing person and take up a new solitary identity elsewhere. But make sure you destroy all dodgy photos of yourself first so your family doesn't choose the most unflattering picture of you to advertise for your whereabouts.**

Don't marry a celebrity or anyone who looks like they have got the potential to become one. If you are undecided about their possible fame factor have it written in the pre-nuptial agreement that they will not become famous or at least not go beyond C-list celeb status.

People tend to respond well to a sound political motive. So if invited anywhere which involves spending money (everywhere then) say you can't go because it goes against your anti-capitalist views. Don't convince them of your argument too strongly as they might decide to stay home with you.

Use novel ways to communicate with people such as smoke signals and semaphore – at least it will be brief as there is only so much you can say with a couple of flags.

When you get home, put on a pair of paint-splattered jeans and if a visitor turns up you are obviously in the middle of painting and it is an inconvenient time for them to come in. Splash a bit of turps over yourself to make it nasally convincing. You will have to be prepared to be embarrassed when they do get their foot in the door and see that your walls are still groaning from 10 years of magnolia anaglypta.

# Install a pay and display machine on your drive.

If in a group discussing musical tastes express your love of the *Sound of Music* soundtrack in order to isolate yourself. But beware of any von Trapp loving octogenarians that may be lurking nearby.

When in company scratch
yourself excessively to
suggest that you have fleas.
Or go to the extreme
measure of trying to catch
fleas from someone else.

Culture values physical attractiveness very highly and so if you are a particularly beautiful social avoider you will have to tolerate more attention than most. It is just as well that beautiful people don't tend to be social avoiders – a generalisation I know, but one that is based on rigorous market research I assure you. Constantly preen yourself, gaze lovingly at any reflective surface you come across e.g., your neighbour's solar-powered roof as nobody likes someone who has too high an opinion of themselves.

Get yourself a really huge, vicious looking dog which looks like it is about to go for the nearest person's ankles at any moment. Of course it will be a big softie really.

Apply for planning permission to build a house on a major flight path where the wind velocity will be sufficient to generate electricity in your home.

If you are a quiet person in company then other people will do most of your social avoiding for you and generally not make too much effort at conversing with you. Your social caution and lack of words will be dismissed as shyness – a lazy generalisation to describe a huge array of personality types.

People tend to socialise more with others who have broadly similar views to themselves on most issues. Therefore be provocative in conversation and always take the opposite view of your companion. For example, if the person is a hygiene fan and they don't go anywhere without their electric toothbrush then you should enthuse about the effectiveness of using your index finger to clean your teeth (just after having cleaned your left nostril with it). Fundamental issues such as this will soon cause a rift between you.

An extreme excuse may be needed to release yourself from certain social occasions. You may need to say that someone close to you has died. But make sure that the prematurely deceased is not guest of honour at the party.

Discharge a good amount of spit when you speak and perfect this so you can aim directly at somebody's eye. It may be necessary to file down your teeth in order to create optimum conditions for projectile emission.

Develop an allergy or medical condition which allows you to opt out any occasion. For any outside gathering the hayfever plea is always accepted with sympathy. If invited somewhere where a certain amount of physical activity will be required such as a bowling party (aagh!) or dancing your bad back prevents you from partaking. Your strict dietary requirements prevent you from going to restaurants as you are allergic to most food substances as well as having difficulties in actually swallowing your food. You are also allergic to perfume which sets off a sneezing fit that can last for days (you may need to perfect a convincing sneeze).

# Have a permanent sign at the end of your drive saying: "WET TARMAC."

Invent a partner whom you have just met and who is whisking you off to romantic locations at the weekends leaving you with no spare time to see anyone. Don't use this if you are already in a relationship – it could cause a few problems.

If you want to write a book, just write a little one so it won't attract too much attention.

Say that you have six different part-time jobs which you work in during unsociable hours. Although people will start to wonder what you actually do with all this money you are making.

People admire academic self-development so a way to dodge social events is to contrive that you are always studying for a qualification and so continually have some exam to revise for or an essay to write. Though people will wonder why you have been unemployed for five years with all those qualifications.

Politely say to your host that you do not wish to spend a prolonged amount of time in their company and there is a high possibility that you will not be asked again. Though it is not inadvisable to cut off everyone from your life in this way as you never know when you might need someone. . .

EMMA
BURGESS

THE LITTLE BOOK OF

**ESSENTIAL
FOREIGN
SWEAR
WORDS**

*summersdale humour*

www.summersdale.com